CELEBRATING THE CITY OF XI'AN

Celebrating the City of Xi'an

Walter the Educator

Silent King Books
A WhichHead Entertainment Imprint

Copyright © 2024 by Walter the Educator

All rights reserved. No part of this book may be reproduced in any manner whatsoever without written per- mission except in the case of brief quotations embodied in critical articles and reviews.

First Printing, 2024

Disclaimer

This book is a literary work; the story is not about specific persons, locations, situations, and/or circumstances unless mentioned in a historical context. Any resemblance to real persons, locations, situations, and/or circumstances is coincidental. This book is for entertainment and informational purposes only. The author and publisher offer this information without warranties expressed or implied. No matter the grounds, neither the author nor the publisher will be accountable for any losses, injuries, or other damages caused by the reader's use of this book. The use of this book acknowledges an understanding and acceptance of this disclaimer.

Celebrating the City of Xi'an is a little collectible souvenir book that belongs to the Celebrating Cities Book Series by Walter the Educator. Collect them all and more books at WaltertheEducator.com

USE THE EXTRA SPACE TO TAKE NOTES AND DOCUMENT YOUR MEMORIES

XI'AN

In the cradle of the ancient Middle Kingdom,

Celebrating the City of Xi'an

Xi'an stands, a timeless marvel, a phoenix risen.

Here the whispers of history weave through air,

Unveiling secrets with every step and stare.

City of endless tales, where emperors once reigned,

Beneath the jade sky, dynasties waxed and waned.

Terracotta warriors in silent vigilance stand,

Guardians of a legacy carved by hand.

Echoes of silk, the ancient road's embrace,

Merchants and travelers from every far-flung place.

Celebrating the City of Xi'an

Lanterns aglow in the twilight's gentle hue,

Illuminating pathways where old meets new.

Xi'an, where the mighty walls still hold their ground,

Encircling stories that forever astound.

The Bell Tower chimes with resonant grace,

Marking time in this storied space.

Celebrating the City of Xi'an

Pagodas reach for heavens, temples in repose,

Offering solace where the lotus grows.

The Big Wild Goose, a symbol of devotion,

Reflects in tranquil water, a scene of pure emotion.

Markets buzz with vibrant life, a sensory delight,

Spices and silks blend in the soft moonlight.

Steaming dumplings, noodles twined with care,

A culinary journey beyond compare.

Muslim Quarter's maze, a cultural fusion,

Harmony in diversity, a seamless inclusion.

Celebrating the City of
Xi'an

Calligraphy dances on scrolls like flowing streams,

Inks and brushes crafting ancient dreams.

Chang'an of yore, a beacon of splendor,

A city of wisdom, a haven to remember.

Confucian ideals and Taoist thought entwine,

Guiding souls through centuries, spirits refined.

In the shadow of the Qinling's rugged might,

Nature and cityscape unite in sight.

Plum blossoms in spring, a fragrant greeting,

Mountains whispering secrets worth repeating.

Celebrating the City of Xi'an

Autumn leaves, a tapestry of golden fire,

Winter's frost, a crystalline choir.

Seasons cycle through this ancient land,

Each adding brushstrokes to a canvas grand.

ABOUT THE CREATOR

Walter the Educator is one of the pseudonyms for Walter Anderson. Formally educated in Chemistry, Business, and Education, he is an educator, an author, a diverse entrepreneur, and he is the son of a disabled war veteran. "Walter the Educator" shares his time between educating and creating. He holds interests and owns several creative projects that entertain, enlighten, enhance, and educate, hoping to inspire and motivate you. Follow, find new works, and stay up to date with Walter the Educator™

at WaltertheEducator.com

www.ingramcontent.com/pod-product-compliance
Lightning Source LLC
LaVergne TN
LVHW012050070526
838201LV00082B/3904